Self-Discipline Mastery

Master Self-Discipline Like a Warrior and Gain Confidence, Motivation, and Happiness!

Table of Contents

Introduction

I want to thank you and congratulate you for purchasing the book, *"Self-Discipline Mastery: Master Self-Discipline Like a Warrior and Gain Confidence, Motivation, and Happiness"*.

Do you have a hard time following through your promises? Do you have a hard time finishing what you have started? Do you make excuses frequently? Are you having difficulty dropping a bad habit like smoking or binge eating? Do you spend more than what you're earning each month? If you answered yes to most of these questions, then you most likely lack self-discipline.

There are many essential characteristics that lead to a person's success, happiness, and self-actualization, but self-discipline is the only quality that guarantees continuing and long-standing success in different facets of life. Self-discipline is crucial in achieving different life goals, whether it is to lose weight, improve your work output, or enhance your financial literacy.

Self-discipline allows you to sacrifice instant pleasure for long term success. Self-discipline or self-control drives you to:

- Work on a business idea even when your enthusiasm is already dwindling.

- Go to the gym even when you do not feel like it.

- Say "no" to fatty foods.

- Wake up early even if all you want to do is lie on your bed all day.

- Limit your Facebook time in order to work on something important.

Self-discipline is rewarding, but it is also challenging. As human beings, we are conditioned to seek instant pleasure. We are conditioned to do what's easy, fun, and convenient. When you practice self-discipline, you are going against your human nature and that's the reason why it's difficult.

This book contains easy-to-follow techniques and strategies that will help you exercise self-discipline. This book contains easy-to-follow steps that will help you achieve everything that you desire – your ideal weight, dream job, and stable financial situation. This book contains strategies, apps, 133 affirmations, and 33 habits that can help strengthen your willpower and self-discipline.

Developing willpower and self-discipline is not easy, but it can make a huge difference in your life. It allows you to control unnecessary impulses and it gives you strength to say "no" to activities that will only distract you from achieving your goals. It gives you the determination to pursue your goals even when the odds are against you.

Thanks again for purchasing this book, I hope you enjoy it!

Chapter 1:
Benefits of Self- Discipline

Self-discipline is a quality or characteristic that will bring you everything that you want in life – money, power, honor, and other forms of material wealth. But aside from this, why do you need to practice self-discipline? What will you get out of it?

1. Focus

Many of us want to have a huge house and a fulfilling career. But, not all of us have the willpower to resist distractions and focus on activities that will help us achieve our dreams. Discipline allows you to focus on activities and action items that will help you achieve your dreams. It helps you resist temptations and distractions.

2. Respect

You'll respect yourself more if you exercise self-discipline and self-control on a regular basis. You'll also earn the respect of your workmates, peers, and even your family.

3. Health

Self-discipline allows you to make healthy choices. It allows you to avoid unhealthy foods such as burger and fries. It also allows you to take your medicine on time.

4. Productivity

Self-discipline allows you to manage distractions more effectively. So, in a sense, it increases your productivity. You'll be able to do more things in a day. Self-discipline gives you clarity and it allows you to effectively manage your time. Self-discipline ensures that you get things done no matter how difficult or inconvenient they may be.

5. Integrity

Self-discipline inspires you to act in line with your values and principles. Living a life of integrity has many benefits. It protects you and it strengthens your confidence. It also sets you apart from other people working in your company.

6. Less Stress

Putting things off can cause stress in the future. So, having the discipline to do important tasks on time helps reduce stress and anxiety. It also allows you to reap the various results of stress reduction such as weight loss, cancer protection, improved sleep, healthier heart, better relationships, a more positive outlook, and a longer life.

7. Ability to Curtail Impulsive Behavior

Self-discipline and self-control help you curb impulsive behaviors such as lying, drug abuse, stealing, binge eating, alcohol abuse, gambling, and overspending. Self-discipline gives you strength to say "no" to habits that may wreak havoc in your life.

8. Improved Chances of Success

Research shows that disciplined people are more likely to get rich because they are able to delay gratification. A study conducted at the University of Pennsylvania shows that people who have self-discipline, self-control, and grit are more successful than those who have genuine talent and intelligence. People who have self-discipline are more likely to finish law or medical school than those who have relevant talents such as critical thinking skills, scientific skills, persuasiveness, logical reasoning, attention to detail, and analytical ability.

9. Increased Level of Happiness

Many think that self-disciplined people are uptight and miserable puritans who miss all the fun. But, the truth is, self-discipline and self-control can make you happier in the long run. According to studies, self-control is not about limiting or depriving yourself. It is about managing opposing and conflicting goals. For example, you'd want to purchase a new Louis Vuitton bag, but you also want to own an eight-bedroom house someday. If you're a self-disciplined person, you will not have any problems letting go of that Louis Vuitton bag for a huge townhouse.

Self-discipline helps increase your chances for success. It also allows you to live responsibly, which would increase the level of your happiness in the long run.

Self-discipline is one of the important keys to living a successful, purposeful, intentional, meaningful, and happy life. It allows you to achieve your biggest hopes and desires.

Chapter 2: Characteristics of Self-Disciplined Achievers

To master self-discipline, you must know what self-disciplined people look like. You must study them closely and mimic their habits and behavior.

Here are the major characteristics of highly disciplined achievers:

- They have a strong and well-defined purpose in life. They know what they want and they are determined to get it.

- They avoid temptation and they have the strength to say "no" to distractions. If they're trying to lose weight, they avoid fatty and sugary foods. If they're trying to save money, they avoid buying clothes or gadgets that they cannot avoid.

- They do not burn themselves out. They rest when they need to.

- They thrive in high-pressure situations.

- They do not give up. They are determined to endure temporary discomfort for long term success.

- They follow through their promises.

- They are proactive.

- They plan ahead.

- They take care of themselves. They are aware that taking care of themselves is an important component of self-discipline.

- They believe in themselves and they have high self-confidence and self-esteem. They do not let anyone bring them down.

- They are willing to learn new skills to achieve their goals.

- They persevere in times of difficulties and adversity.

- They are self-assured.

- They can withstand physical, mental, and emotional challenges.

- They have the ability to visualize success.

- They have the ability to plan and organize.

- They study other highly disciplined people for learning and inspiration.

- They find pleasure in working towards their goals.

- They have unwavering commitment to their goals.

- They are patient. They know that success does not happen overnight.

Take note of these characteristics and learn to practice them on a daily basis. Below is a chart that will help you mimic the characteristics of highly disciplined achievers. We will discuss some of these action items in detail later in this book.

Characteristics	Action Items
Strong sense of purpose	Set goals and discover your inner desires.
Follow through promises	Honor your word.
Self-care	Eat right and exercise regularly.
Grit	Do not give up even when faced with difficulties.

Willing to learn	Attend classes and seminars that will strengthen your skills and help you achieve your goals.
Self-confidence	Silence your inner critic and make it a habit to say affirmations daily to strengthen your self-confidence and self-esteem.
Planning ahead	Plan for your future. Set long term and short term goals.

Mental endurance	Force yourself to do something even when you don't feel like it.
Ability to visualize success	Spend 10 to 15 minutes a day thinking about how it feels like to achieve your goals. Visualization will condition and motivate you to take the necessary steps to achieve your dreams.
Proactive	You have to take responsibility for your life and do what is necessary to achieve your dreams.

Commitment, Determination, and Perseverance	Keep your eye on the prize. Always remind yourself that your future and your dreams are at stake here. This will give you strength to endure challenges, discomfort, and difficulties.
Ability to Avoid Temptation	You must avoid temptation at all cost. If you're a drug addict, avoid fellow junkies and associate yourself with sober and successful people. If you're trying to lose weight, avoid pastry shops at all cost.

Patience	It takes time to achieve your goals so you have to be patient. Recognize your impatience pattern and slowly transform impatience into patience. Always remind yourself that the reward that you will get after you've reached your goal is worth the wait.

As mentioned earlier, we will discuss the details of these action items in the later chapters of this book but you can print the table above and use it as a guide.

Chapter 3:
The Science of Self -Discipline

Earlier in this book, we defined self-discipline (also known as self-control, willpower, and inner strength) as the stamina to persevere and withstand any problems and discomfort just to achieve a specific goal. It is the ability to delay gratification and control unnecessary impulses in order to achieve something greater. It is the power to overcome procrastination and laziness. It is also known as inner strength or self-control.

According to experts, willpower or self-discipline is a limited resource that could deplete over time. According to Dr. Roy Baumeister of the Florida State University, willpower not only depends on psychological and mental strength but also on physiological factors such as the blood glucose level. Your willpower also gets depleted when you exercise self-control too often. For example, if you exercise self-control more often, you may feel that you deserve a reward.

In a study conducted in 1998. Researchers studied two groups of people. They placed these people in separate rooms and put chocolate on a table in front of the research respondents. They allowed one group to eat the chocolate and asked the second group to merely look at the chocolate. An hour later, they asked both groups to solve the same puzzle. The results show that people who resisted the temptation to eat the chocolates are having difficulties in solving the puzzle.

When you're stressed, worn out, sad, depressed, lonely, or you've been exercising self-control for too long, it will be harder for you to exercise self-discipline and self-control. So, here are some tips to avoid willpower depletion and continue to exercise willpower and self-discipline for a long period of time:

Stabilize your blood sugar level.

As mentioned earlier, low blood sugar level is closely associated with low self-discipline. But, blood sugar spikes caused by sugary food items (such as soda) could backfire and cause a huge drop in the blood sugar level later on. To strengthen your willpower and self-discipline, you have to practice the following sugar-stabilizing tips:

- Eat breakfast.

- Eat snacks in between meals.

- Include protein in every meal.

- Avoid sodas and packaged fruit juices.

- Avoid coffee, cigarettes, and other stimulants.

Sleep at least eight hours a night.

Sleep deprivation can weaken your body and mind. It can weaken your willpower, too. So, in order to improve your willpower, you have to sleep at least eight hours every night. If you have a hard time sleeping, the following tips may be helpful:

- Maintain your body's natural rhythm and try to sleep and wake up at the same time each day.

- Cut down your caffeine consumption. It is also best to avoid drinking soda or anything with caffeine at least three hours before bedtime.

- Do not eat too much at night. Eating fatty foods can cause digestive problems and heartburn that may keep you awake at night.

- Clear your head and try to empty your worries.

- Keep the noise down.

- Keep your bedroom cool and make sure that your bed is clean and comfortable.

- If you work from home, do not work in your bedroom. This way, you will be able to mentally associate your bedroom with sleep.

- Take a warm bath before sleeping. This will help relax your body.

- If you're working nightshift, use room-darkening shades.

Manage your stress.

According to studies, stress weakens your willpower. If you're stressed, it will be difficult for you to resist temptation. So, to strengthen your willpower, you need to learn how to manage your stress.

Address the root causes of your stress. Think about the pros and cons.

- Maintain a positive attitude. Accept that there are things that you cannot control.

- Try breathing exercises when faced with a difficult situation.

- Eat healthy food to avoid sugar spikes.

- Learn how to say no. Avoid spreading yourself too thin.

- Manage your time wisely to avoid cramming.

- Limit your caffeine and alcohol intake.

- Aim to do your best all the time.

- Stay away from stress or anxiety triggers.

- Get help if necessary. If you feel that your stress is getting out of hand, then it's time to seek professional health.

Enjoy life.

Positive experiences help replenish your willpower reserve. So, to strengthen your willpower and self-discipline, it is necessary to take a few moments to simply enjoy life and its small pleasures. Here are 50 ways to enjoy life and strengthen your self-control in the process.

- Allow yourself to be lazy even just for a day.

- Read comic books or romance novels.

- Sing your heart out in a karaoke bar. You can even sing in the shower.

- Call a friend that you have not seen for a long time.

- Give yourself a gift.

- Go to a pet shop and watch the cute critters.

- Watch the sunrise and sunset.

- Start planning your fantasy vacation.

- Read poetry.

- Step out and dance in the rain.

- Cook a great meal for your loved ones.

- Learn how to play a musical instrument.

- Live in the present.

- Make big celebrations for small achievements.

- Spread good vibes.

- Write a diary.

- Help another person out.

- Read old love letters.

- Read inspirational quotes.

- Eat chocolate every now and then.

- Always follow the golden rule. This will save you from stress and protect you from negative feelings such as guilt.

- Fly a kite.

- Plant herbs in your backyard.

- Watch your favorite movies.

- Trade ideas with like-minded people.

- Learn a new skill.

- Run around your neighborhood or join a marathon.

- Learn a new language.

- Go kayaking.

- Join a fun walk with your friends.

- Watch a play.

- Bike around your neighborhood.

- Keep a journal.

- Surround yourself with people who make you laugh.

- Shop for good clothes.

- Go swimming with your loved ones.

- Try something new.

- Watch funny films and TV series.

- Live for others.

- Spend time with your favorite people.

- Gaze at the stars.

- Drink cheap beer with your friends and favorite colleagues after a long day.

- Read and write poetry.

- Dance like no one's watching.

- Go rollerblading.

- Start completing your bucket list.

- Play in the snow.

- Wink at strangers just for fun.

- Listen to good music.

- Learn how to cook your favorite restaurant dish.

Rewarding yourself with the little pleasures in life would help strengthen your willpower and self-discipline. It will make it easier for you to give up bad habits and instant pleasure for bigger, grander, and more sustainable rewards.

Take care of yourself.

Self-care improves your health and the level of your happiness. It also strengthens your willpower. Studies show that people who practice self-care regularly find it easier to practice self-discipline and self- control.

- Eat healthy and well-balanced meals.

- Take a bath daily.

- Establish your own personal boundaries and call out people who cross them.

- Do things that you are passionate about.

- Learn to take compliments gracefully.

- Surround yourself with scents that help you relax. Spray lavender, ylang ylang, or rosemary scents in your room.

- Rest when you need to.

- Get enough sleep. When you're sleep deprived, it will be difficult for you to delay gratification and do things that are necessary in order to achieve your goals.

- Read a good book. This is good for your mind and soul.

- Make time for fun and play.

Remember that your willpower supply is not infinite. You will experience willpower or ego depletion if you push yourself too hard. So, you need to strengthen your willpower by living a balanced life. Working too hard will drain you eventually, so it's best to do fun things from time to time.

Chapter 4:
Set Clear Goals

To strengthen your willpower and self-discipline, you need strong motivation; and to keep yourself motivated, you have to set goals. Goals give you a strong sense of purpose. It gives you clear focus and it allows you to use your resources and time wisely. It helps you make a good decision and it also helps you achieve peace of mind.

Tie your goals to your inner desires.

In order to stay motivated, you have to set goals that truly motivate you. Set goals that excite you. If you'll set goals just to please other people, you are setting yourself up for failure. Remember that your willpower is a limited resource. So, to ensure that you sustain your enthusiasm and motivation until you achieve your goal, you have to set goals that are truly important to you. You have to set goals that will truly change your life.

Set SMART goals.

To increase your chances of achieving your objectives, you have to set SMART (specific, measurable, achievable, relevant, time-bound) goals. Vague goals do not provide enough sense of direction, so it is important to set specific, clear, and well-defined goals. It is also important to include deadlines, precise amounts in your goals. This way, you can measure your degree of achievement or success. If your goal is simply to "save money", how will you know if you are closer to achieving your goal? If you have saved a dollar, is that enough?

It is also important to set goals that are achievable. If you set goals that are impossible to achieve, you are setting yourself up for failure. You'll also end up demoralizing yourself and this could negatively affect your self-confidence and self-esteem in the long run. Your goals must also be congruent with the direction that you want to take. This will give you laser-like focus.

Lastly, it is important to set a deadline. A goal without a deadline is weak. Setting a deadline will create a strong sense of urgency and will inspire you to take action right away.

Write your goals.

Written goals are a hundred times more powerful and compelling than unwritten goals. So, it is important to put your goals in writing. Write all your goals in a notebook and call this a "Goal Book". Make sure to write one goal per page so you can also write your progress on each page later on.

If you're the techie type, you can use goal setting apps such as:

- Nozbe

This app will allow you to track your goals, daily tasks, and habits. This goal tracking app is also a great task management system and you can tie it to your Dropbox or Evernote account.

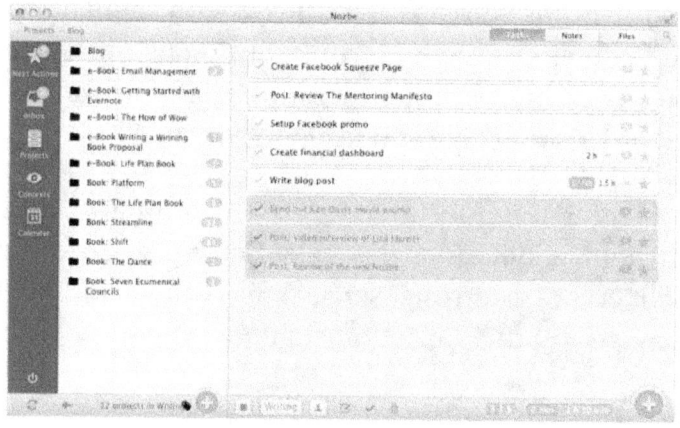

Photo Source: michaelhyatt.com

- GoalsOnTrack

This is one of the most popular goal-setting devices today. It helps you record your goal and the purpose of each goal. You can also enter the start date, goal achievement date, subgoals, metrics, habits, and action plan.

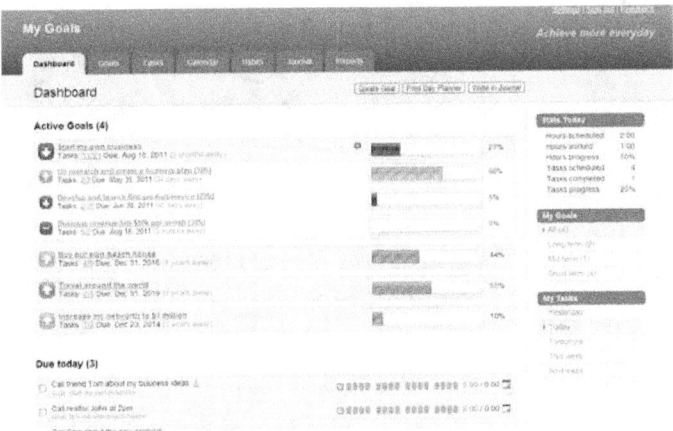

Photo Source: goalsontrack.com

- Strides

This is a well-designed app that helps you track goals and habits. It helps you track your goals and keep yourself motivated to continue working on these goals.

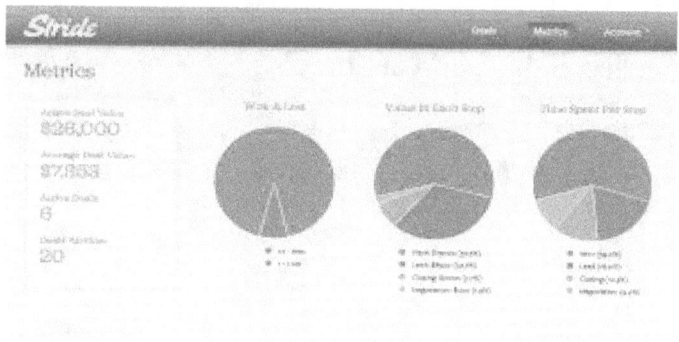

Photo Source: techcrunch.com

- LifeTick

LifeTick is more than just a goal-setting app. It also helps you define your core values. It allows you to focus on what's important to you. It makes it easier for you to define your "area of focus". Moreover, this app allows you to create a date-sequenced journal of all your tasks and goal-related activities.

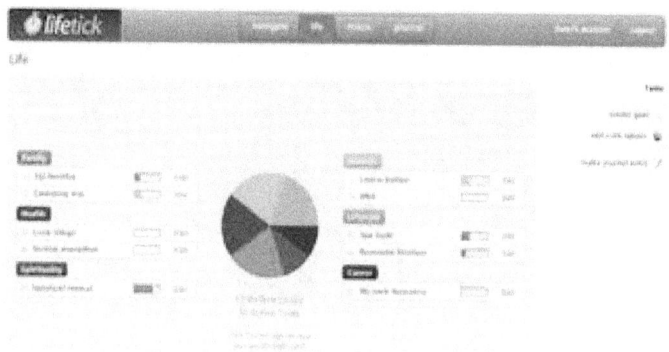

Photo Source: Unclutterer.com

Set goals for every area of your life.

To ensure that you are moving forward, it is necessary to set goals in every area of your life including finances, career, relationship, and personal development. This will ensure that you will enjoy success in different aspects of your life. Here are some career ideas that you can use in setting different life goals:

Financial Goals

- Get out of debt within a year.

- Plan for early retirement.

- Have a $20,000 emergency fund.

- Have a perfect credit score (850) within two years.

- Pay off the mortgage in 5 years.

- Pay for a car in cash in 3 years.

- Pay off the student loans in 2 years.

Career Goals

- Learn a new skill.

- Create a website for your business.

- Stop micromanaging your employees.

- Ask for a raise.

- Get a promotion within a year.

- Turn your passion into a business.

- Be an industry expert.

- Increase performance metrics and review marks.

Personal Development

- Be more confident.

- Rise at 5:00 am daily.

- Read at least one personal development book a month.

- Be more optimistic.

- Manage your time more efficiently.

- Make more friends.

- Strengthen your spirituality through meditation and worship.

Relationship Goals

- Reconnect with all friends.

- Go on a lunch date with your parents at least twice a month.

- Get married and have kids.

Setting goals in every aspect of your life will allow you to enjoy happiness and success in your career, relationships, and finances. It also allows you to be the version of yourself.

Set long-term and short-term goals.

A short-term goal is something that you want to accomplish in twelve months or less. Short-term goals are usually easy to accomplish and do not require long-term commitment. These goals help create a momentum and boost your self-confidence. These goals also allow you to enjoy quick and instant results. Here are some examples of short-term goals:

- Go to work on time every day for the next 30 days.

- Keep breaks at minimum.

- Set aside $10 per day for your travel fun.

- Read one book every week.

- Workout for at least 30 minutes every day.

- Get a personal trainer.

- Lose 5 pounds.

- Pay the bills by the end of the week.

- Meet the project deadline.

A long-term goal is something that you want to accomplish in the future. Long term goals give you a strong sense of purpose. It helps you achieve something great in the long run and it makes your life more exciting. Here are some examples of long-term goals:

- Be a lawyer.

- Get a master's degree.

- Retire before 60.

- Buy a house.

Short-term goals are also sometimes stepping stones that will help you achieve long-term goals. It is important to set both short-term and long-term goals because long-term goals give you a strong sense of direction, while short-term goals give a great sense of achievement.

Create action plans.

Remember that goal-setting is not enough. If you want to wield your self-discipline and achieve your goals, you have to create action plans. Action plans help you channel your time, resource, and skills to reach goals. These action items create a sense of urgency and it strengthens your commitment to your goals.

Setting smart goals will not only increase your motivation, willpower, self-control, and self-discipline. It also helps you prioritize and manage your resources. Having goals trains you to manage your time more effectively. It obliges you to take the necessary action to live a life that you are proud of. It gives you fulfillment and it inspires you to use your God-given talent and intelligence to achieve the things that matter to you.

Chapter 5:
Just Do It

One way to master self-discipline is to habitually beat procrastination. Procrastination can destroy your life in many ways. It robs you of precious time and opportunities. It prevents you from taking the first step towards your dreams and it can potentially ruin your career as it keeps you from meeting deadlines and hitting targets. It leads to poor decisions and it decreases your self-esteem over time. It also destroys your reputation.

Here are the signs that you are a procrastinator and you have low self-discipline:

- Prioritizing emails and social media over important tasks.

- Saying "yes" to unimportant tasks.

- Excessive daydreaming at work.

- Setting unreasonable and vague goals.

- Constantly making excuses.

- Avoiding the discomfort of doing an unpleasant or difficult task.

- Waiting for everything to be perfect before doing a task.

To master the virtue of self-discipline, you must overcome procrastination. Here are some valuable tips that will help you overcome procrastination and practice self-discipline and self-control on a daily basis:

Get to the bottom of it.

To beat procrastination, you have to identify the root cause of your procrastinating behavior and lack of self-discipline. Do you skip tasks simply because you're not in the mood? Are you afraid of failure? Are you afraid of success? Do you skip tasks that bore you? Are you indecisive or are you a perfectionist? Are you afraid that you'll screw it up or are you just plain lazy?

When you get to the bottom of your procrastinating behavior, it will be easier for you to deal with it and devise strategies that help eliminate the root cause of the problem.

Believe in yourself.

To beat procrastination and strengthen your willpower, you must believe in yourself. You must believe that you can do the task at hand, no matter how difficult it may seem. Learn to trust yourself. Silence your inner critic by replacing negative thoughts with positive ones. Stop bullying yourself and start to be your own number-one fan. Whenever you hear yourself saying "I can't do this", quickly replace that with an empowering thought such as "This is hard, but I'm going to do this" or "There's no harm in trying". Doing this will give you the strength to tackle the important task at hand.

Organize your workspace.

It is easy to procrastinate if you have a messy workspace. So, make it a habit to organize your workspace. Purge your office and get rid of things that you no longer want or need. Then, organize your files and office supplies by grouping similar documents and things together. It is also good to buy a good labeler and label your shelves, drawers, containers, folders, and cabinets. This way, it will be easier for you to find things.

Create a "to do" list and stick to it.

A "to do" list helps create order. It helps manage your tasks more effectively. It helps you organize your time and it gives you a strong sense of accountability. To strengthen your self-discipline and overcome procrastination, you must create a "to do" list.

Write down three important tasks in your to-do list daily and prioritize them by importance.

Use index cards in writing your "to do" list and write one task on each card. This will allow you to focus on one task at a time. If this system does not work for you, you can try electronic time organizers such as Evernote, Any.Do, Todoist, Wunderlist, Pocket Lists, and Calvetica.

Do the most difficult, important, and time-consuming task first. This way, you'll feel a strong sense of accomplishment even if you're able to complete only one task.

Use your energy wisely.

Assign time estimates and try to stick to it. This will enable you to manage your time more effectively. This will also allow you to say "no" to tasks that you cannot complete during the day.

Write your "to do" list the night before so you won't forget anything.

Use the Eisenhower's Urgent/Important Principle – a time management tool, in prioritizing your tasks by urgency and importance. According to Dr. Eisenhower, not all urgent things are important and not all important things are urgent. So, to determine which tasks to prioritize, delegate, or delete from your list, simply refer to the matrix below:

URGENT & IMPORTANT

1

crises
meaningful deadlines
emergencies

IMPORTANT
NOT URGENT

2

relationships
health
reflection & planning

URGENT
NOT IMPORTANT

3

interruptions
email
meetings

NOT URGENT
NOT IMPORTANT

4

trivia
time-wasters
busywork

Photo Source: tumblr.com

Prioritizing your tasks will allow you to focus on important and urgent things. It allows you to manage your time well and do tasks that are essential in achieving your goals and dreams.

You can be flexible from time to time. But, to strengthen your self-discipline, you have to stick to your list most of the time and do the tasks that you say you will do.

Give yourself a small reward.

Sometimes, you have to reward yourself with small treats to get yourself to do important tasks. For example, you can promise yourself a small cheese tart if you complete an important task.

Finally, drop all your excuses. Write down all your excuses and burn it. If you want to be a highly disciplined achiever, you must replace all your excuses with positive, empowering, and more realistic thoughts.

Excuses	Fact
I do not have enough time.	We all have 24 hours a day. If you want to achieve something great, you have to make time for it. You have to prioritize it.
It's too hard.	You will not move forward in life if you routinely choose to do easy and more convenient tasks. You must do whatever it takes to achieve your goals.
I am too young.	Mark Zuckerberg was only 19 when he launched Facebook. So you can work on your goals, no matter how

	young you are.
I am too old.	Colonel Sanders founded Kentucky Fried Chicken when he was 65 years old. So, you're not too old to start a business or follow your passion. Morgan Freeman became an international star when he was 52. Mark Twain wrote his amazing novel Huckleberry Finn when he was already 49 years old.
I am too tired.	If you want something bad enough, you must do whatever it takes to achieve it. Marissa Mayer, Yahoo CEO, worked for 130 hours per week while she is at Google. Elon Musk also works 100 hours a week.

	Sometimes, you must do some important tasks even if you're tired.
I do not have enough money.	Many people have started their business without capital. If you have a great idea, all you need to do is find a good venture capitalist to help turn your idea into a lucrative business.
I do not have enough talent. I am not smart enough to do that stuff.	According to Angela Lee Duckworth, a famous psychologist, grit is more important than talent. Grit allows you to learn just about anything from writing, singing, playing an instrument, or baking a perfect fondant cake. You do not have to be born with talent or intelligence to be

	successful.
I am too busy.	You must learn to prioritize important tasks. This means that you must constantly say "no" to tasks and activities that are not important.
I do not have enough support. People tell me that I cannot do it.	You must learn to tune out negative people. If you can't do that, then stay away from them. Surround yourself with people who love you and support you.
I do not know how to do that.	You can learn to do just about anything you set your mind into. You can learn how to code, play an instrument, or write poems.

I can't beat other people.	The only person you should be competing is yourself. To master discipline, you must focus on beating your own record to become a better person.
What if I fail?	So what if you fail? Many people failed a hundred times before they became successful. Bill Gates' first business, Traf-O-Data, failed. Colonel Sanders' fried chicken recipe was rejected more than one thousand times before a restaurant accepted it. Albert Einstein was expelled from school and he was rejected by the Zurich Polytechnic School. Failure is not necessarily a bad thing. It strengthens you and

	teaches you valuable lessons that you need to succeed.

To master self-discipline and eliminate your procrastinating behavior, you must drop all your excuses and "just do" it.

Chapter 6:
Mastering the Ultimate Self-Discipline Strategies

Self-discipline is something that you will never acquire overnight. It takes days, months, and even years of practice. Setting goals and dropping procrastinating behavior is not enough. To master self-discipline and strengthen your willpower, you have to practice the following strategies:

Acknowledge Your Weaknesses

To master self-discipline, you must acknowledge your weaknesses. Do you have a hard time shutting down Facebook and other distracting accounts? Are you impatient? Are you stubborn or uncompromising? Are you reluctant to delegate tasks? Are you too sensitive? Do you have a hard time working in a team? These weaknesses might get in the way of mastering self-discipline so you have to take time to sit down and identify your weaknesses.

Ignoring your weaknesses may ruin your work performance so you have to admit that you're not perfect. Owning and facing your weaknesses helps you maximize your potential. It gives you an opportunity to turn these weaknesses into strengths. Write down all your weaknesses on a piece of paper and devise a plan on how to transform these weaknesses into strengths.

Delay Gratification

Delaying gratification has its benefits. It helps you appreciate what you have more. It teaches you the value of hard work. It helps build mental strength and discipline.

A study conducted in the 1970s by Walter Mischel showed that people who are able to delay gratification are more likely to succeed in life. In an experiment, Dr. Mischel placed a plate full of cookies in front of children. He told the children to wait for a few minutes and promised a reward for those who can wait. Some children ate the cookies after Mischel left the room, but a few were able to resist the urge. The children who were able to delay gratification have better grades in school and fewer behavioral problems than those who ate the cookies right away.

The ability to delay gratification is essential in becoming a high disciplined achiever. Here are some strategies that will help you avoid the lures of instant gratification:

1. Remind yourself of your goals.

Always remind yourself that there's something greater waiting for you at the end of the tunnel. Would you trade your lung health for the pleasure of smoking two packs of cigarette each day? Would you give up the opportunity to travel around the world for an expensive designer bag? Are you willing to trade your beautiful and slim body for several slices of blueberry cheesecake? If you constantly remind yourself of your goals, it will be easier for you to delay gratification.

2. Surround yourself with self-disciplined people.

To master self-discipline, you must surround yourself with highly-disciplined people. Surround yourself with people who support you in achieving your goals. For example, if you're trying to lose weight and avoid eating dessert, surround yourself with people who have healthy eating habits.

3. Prioritize long term goals.

You must prioritize your long term goals over instant pleasure at all times. Whenever you're about to give in, always remind yourself of your principles, values, and long term goals.

4. Reward yourself.

Each time you are able to delay gratification, give yourself a reward. This will increase your motivation to practice self-discipline regularly.

Remove Temptations

The best way to avoid temptations is to remove temptations. As what they say - out of sight, out of mind. As mentioned earlier, your willpower is limited, so be careful not to waste it. Each time you say "no" to a temptation in front of you, you are depleting your willpower. So, as much as possible, remove all temptations from your life. For example, if you know you can't resist designer bags, do not go to designer stores. If you know that you watch TV too much, remove the television in your bedroom or cancel your cable subscription. If it's hard for you to resist junk food, do not keep any in your house.

Learn to Delegate

You do not have to do everything. To strengthen your willpower and master self-discipline, you must prioritize tasks that help you achieve your goals, so it's best to delegate menial tasks. You can hire a virtual assistant or simply ask someone to do it for you.

Meditation

Meditation strengthens self-discipline. It gives you the inner strength to delay gratification. It also activated the "willpower" part of your brain. According to a study conducted at Caltech in 2009, the dorsolateral prefrontal cortex of your brain is activated in highly disciplined achievers. It also happens that this part of the brain is active during meditation. Meditation also releases brain chemicals like dopamine and endorphins that help reduce your cravings. So, take time to meditate at least 10 to 15 minutes a day.

Break it Down

Many people are overwhelmed with big tasks, so it is important to break down big tasks into smaller tasks. For example, if your task is to write a thesis, break it down into the following smaller tasks:

- Pick a thesis topic.

- Research on the topic.

- Pick a title and write the introduction.

- Write the chapters (problem, background, methodology of the study, etc.).

- Write the conclusion.

When you break down your big tasks into smaller tasks, it will be easier for you to get things done.

Get Digital

You can use many computer and mobile apps to practice self-control and self-discipline, including:

- SelfControl – This app will help you block distracting websites for a specific amount of time. As of writing, this app is available for Mac users only.

- TrackTime – This system, as the name suggests, allows you to track the time that you're spending on the computer.

- FocusBooster – This app helps you focus on one single task for 25 minutes.

- Way of Life – According to personal development experts, it takes 21 days to build a habit. This app will help you practice self-control and self-discipline for 21 days.

- Lift – This will help you focus on a personal resolution (exercise daily) or business goal (increase leads).

- Mint – This app helps you create a budget. So, if you're trying to spend within your means, this is the best app for you.

In order to master self-discipline and live a great life, you have to regularly choose to practice self-control. You must be able to tolerate emotional discomfort and delay gratification for a long period of time. You must be able to sacrifice temporary pleasure and comfort for long-term success.

Chapter 6:
Motivate Yourself

Practicing self-control and self-discipline is not an easy feat so you must be motivated at all times. Here are some techniques that will help you stay motivated for a long time.

Visualization

Visualization is a powerful tool that will help you achieve whatever you want in life. It tricks your subconscious mind into commanding your body to do whatever it takes to achieve your goals and dreams. Visualization increases your confidence and it strengthens your willpower. It helps you beat stress, depression, and anxiety, too.

Every day, sit down and close your eyes. Then, imagine that you have already achieved what you want. Imagine yourself having that ideal bikini body. Imagine that you are already a successful entrepreneur. You have to visualize every detail and heighten all your senses when visualizing success to reap the maximum benefits of visualization.

Celebrate Small Wins

To keep yourself motivated, you must celebrate small wins. You can give yourself a small treat after you have completed a complicated task. You can take a field trip to fascinating places such as beaches and museums after a long and grueling work week. You can also buy yourself a bouquet of flower. You can also get out of town or take a class.

Rewarding yourself keeps you motivated and it keeps you on the right track. It helps you focused on work and helps strengthen your willpower and self-discipline.

Affirmations

Affirmations encourage and motivate you to do whatever it takes to achieve your dreams. These give you the confidence to take on more challenging tasks. They also give you the inner peace necessary to endure challenges and difficulties. Here are 133 affirmations that you can use daily to strengthen your willpower and self-confidence.

My willpower is improving every day.

- I can control my habits.

- I will do whatever I set my mind into.

- I honor my word.

- I always follow through my goals.

- My willpower is growing stronger every day.

- I am above all temptations.

- I am in control of my life.

- I am disciplined.

- I am in charge of my actions.

- I always put my best efforts in everything I do.

- I make wise choices.

- I do not wait until I feel like it.

- I finish what I start.

- I do not make excuses.

- I do not let anyone pull me down.

- I am a man/woman of character.

- I can easily handle temptations.

- I control my thoughts.

- I do whatever I need to do to make my life better.

- I can control my habits.

- I have strong self-control.

- I am a winner.

- I have strong willpower.

- I refuse to quit.

- Giving up is not an option.

- I take full responsibility for my actions.

- I have an amazing inner strength.

- I have the capability to resist all temptations.

- I have a strong will to succeed.

- I take responsibility for my choices and actions.

- I am proactive.

- My will is powerful.

- Nothing can stop me from living my dream life.

- I have infinite willpower.

- I get going even when the going gets tough.

- My self-control is growing every day.

- I have complete control over myself.

- I am committed to my goals.

- Self-discipline is natural to me.

- I work hard every day to strengthen my willpower.

- I am focused on achieving my goals.

- I can easily resist temptation.

- I work hard to achieve my goals.

- I am persistent.

- I am strong.

- I will and I can.

- I am the master of my life.

- I am full of self-discipline.

- I choose to delay gratification to achieve my dreams.

- I have a rock solid willpower.

- I take responsibility for my actions.

- I am in complete control of myself.

- I have dedicated to success.

- I have an iron will.

- I can control my cravings.

- I honor my highest intentions.

- I let all the distractions go.

- I am willing to delay instant pleasure for greater rewards.

- I can delay gratification.

- Self-discipline is the key to success.

- I am motivated and energized.

- I achieve my goals effortlessly.

- I know what I want and I am not afraid to go for it.

- I eliminate helplessness.

- I take charge of my life.

- I have amazing inner strength.

- My mind is strong.

- I have complete control over myself.

- I am highly disciplined.

- I am dedicated to achieving my goals.

- I have a strong mind.

- I have an unshakable determination.

- My willpower is strong enough to move mountains.

- I will persevere even when faced with difficulties.

- I will never give up.

- I take responsibility for my actions.

- Failures strengthen my determination to keep going no matter what.

- I can easily turn setbacks into comebacks.

- I am patient, persistent, and productive.

- Giving up is not an option for me.

- My persistence and self-discipline protects me from small everyday distractions.

- I persist even when faced with obstacles.

- I keep on going until I achieve my goals.

- I am strong and resilient.

- I am persistent.

- I am always moving forward.

- I tell others what I want.

- Rejection makes me stronger.

- I am a hard worker.

- I am strong enough to overcome all the problems that are thrown my way.

- I am fearless.

- I am a persistent and determined person.

- I am determined to achieve all my goals.

- I am inspired and motivated to live the life of my dreams.

- I am strong-willed.

- I am focused.

- I am reliable and persistent.

- I am determined to win.

- I am getting closer to my goals.

- I push myself further every day.

- I am diligent.

- I am a survivor.

- I am unstoppable.

- I demand the best from myself.

- I am in control of my life.

- I always go the extra mile to achieve my goal.

- I have the willpower and self-discipline to overcome all my problems and obstacles.

- My willpower is unshakeable.

- Self- control is easy for me.

- I can control my emotions.

- I do not make unnecessary decisions.

- I acknowledge my weaknesses.

- I am determined to achieve my goals.

- I am willing to do uncomfortable things just to achieve my goals.

- I am awesome.

- I am disciplined.

- I am stronger.

- I do not procrastinate.

- I take action.

- I can delay gratification.

- I have strong self-control.

- I am the master of my destiny.

- I am driven and passionate.

- I can achieve great things.

- I have a clear plan.

- I can handle emotional discomfort.

- I have the discipline to accomplish my goals.

- I am determined to achieve my dreams.

- I get things done.

- I can do this.

- I choose to take action.

- I will do whatever it takes to fulfill my dreams.

Keeping yourself motivated helps strengthen your self-control and it helps you do whatever it is that you need to do to achieve everything that you want in life.

Chapter 8:
Daily Choices That Help Strengthen Your Willpower and Self-discipline

Self-discipline is not something that you can develop in one day. It takes constant practice. Practicing self-discipline is a choice that you have to make every day. Here are some practical tips that allows you to practice self-control and self-discipline daily:

- Maintain a good posture.

- Hold your tongue when you are about to yell or say something unpleasant.

- Eat vegetables instead of junk foods.

- Make a decision not to store junk food in your home.

- Resist the urge to eat desert.

- If you're still studying, read at least one chapter of your textbook every day.

- Save at least $100 per week for your emergency fund.

- Meditate for at least 10 minutes a day.

- Do a task even when you're not in the mood.

- Try to endure a little hunger.

- Talk to someone about a topic that makes you uncomfortable. Do not try to avoid difficult situations.

- Pay yourself first and then spend the rest.

- Before you buy something, ask yourself "Do I really need this?"

- Create a weekly budget and stick to it.

- Say "no" to excuses.

- Do not bring your credit card to work.

- Pay for your groceries in cash.

- Pay your bills on time.

- Try your best to meet deadlines.

- Resist the urge to drink soda and high calorie drinks.

- Pay attention to your food portion.

- Make a meal plan and stick to it.

- Wash dishes right after eating.

- Limit your TV time to 30 minutes a day.

- Block Facebook and other distracting websites during work time. You can use the SelfControl app to block your own access to social networking sites.

- Think before you act and before you say anything.

- Wake up at 5 am every day.

- Run for at least 20 minutes daily.

- Practice gratitude for what you have. This will keep you from buying more things.

- Make your bed every morning.

- Create a morning routine and stick to it.

- Be silent if you have nothing good to say. Remember what they say, "do not do something permanently foolish just because you are temporarily angry".

These activities allow you to exercise your willpower and eventually master the art of self-discipline. To strengthen your willpower and master self-discipline, you have to practice it every day in all aspects of your life – career, personal development, finances, and even relationships.

Conclusion

Thank you again for purchasing this book!

I hope this book was able to help you master self-discipline and achieve your life goals. I hope that the tips and strategies in this book were able to help you build a more successful and happier life.

The next step is to keep on doing these tips and techniques. Remember that mastering self-discipline is a life-long journey. You can also share this book to friends and family who also need to make a huge change in their lives.

Finally, if you enjoyed this book, then I'd like to ask you for a favor, would you be kind enough to leave a review for this book on Amazon? It'd be greatly appreciated!

Thank you and good luck!